LEAST THINGS

Poems About Small Natures

by

Photographs by
Jason Stemple

Wordsong ❖ Boyds Mills Press

Nature excels in the least things. *(In minimis Natura praestat.)*
—Pliny the Elder

To our newest "least thing," David Francis
Stemple, born August 6, 2002
—J. Y.

To my "least things," Caroline and Amelia
—J. S.

Text copyright © 2003 by Jane Yolen
Photographs copyright © 2003 by Jason Stemple
All rights reserved

Published by Wordsong
Boyds Mills Press, Inc.
A Highlights Company
815 Church Street
Honesdale, Pennsylvania 18431
Printed in China

Publisher Cataloging-in-Publication Data (U.S.)

Yolen, Jane.
   Least things : poems about small natures / by Jane Yolen ;
photographs by Jason Stemple.—1st ed.
[32] p. : col. ill. ; cm.

Summary: Photographs and haiku about small creatures
in nature, such as the spider, snail, hummingbird,
grasshopper, and crab.
ISBN 1-59078-098-1
1. Nature—Juvenile poetry. 2. Children's poetry,
American. (1. Nature—Poetry. 2. American poetry
—Collections.)
I. Stemple, Jason. II. Title.
811.54 21   PS3575.O43L43 2003
2002117195

First edition, 2003
Book designed by Jason Thorne
The text of this book is set in 19-point Palatino.

Visit our Web site at www.boydsmillspress.com

10 9 8 7 6 5 4 3 2 1

Contents

A Note from the Author

A long time ago I came upon the quotation "Nature excels in the least things." Henry David Thoreau, the great American writer and philosopher, wrote it in his journal on January 14, 1861. He attributed it to Pliny the Elder, a noted military officer and naturalist who lived in ancient Rome.

How wonderful, I thought, having just had my first granddaughter and feeling my particular "least thing" was splendid indeed. I decided at that moment to collaborate with my photographer son Jason Stemple on a collection of poems and photographs, using "Least Things" as the title.

During the years that followed, Jason and I kept working on photos and poems of small (least) things in nature. But neither of us was pleased with the results. He had a picture of snails we loved, and I wrote a long poem to go with it that we both disliked. He'd taken a photograph of a miniature crab that delighted me, but I couldn't come up with a poem at all.

Books—even small books—take a long time.

Slowly, Jason's pile of photographs about the smallest things in nature grew. (Well, the pile grew, not the small things!) But the poems I tried to write did not work. They simply overwhelmed their tiny subjects.

Then one night I sat up in bed. I had been dreaming about the book. In my dream, all the poems were haiku. Of course! How could I have been so slow to realize that the haiku—a Japanese form of poetry that celebrates nature usually in three lines of five, seven, and five syllables—was the perfect way to write these poems. After that, the poetry tumbled out, matching the ever-growing piles of pictures.

— Jane Yolen

P.S. That original "least thing" grandbaby—Maddison Jane Piatt—is now quite grown up at eight years old, as is her cousin Alison Isabelle Stemple at four. But there is a new "least thing"—a grandson, just born—and so this book is dedicated to him.

5

Snail

I make my slow way
Between the water droplets,
Between the minutes.

snail

The body of the snail is moist and slimy. It has a single foot, which is a creeping organ. When frightened, the snail pulls itself into its shell.

crab

The crab's body is covered by a shell, which is also its skeleton. It has jointed legs and often moves by crawling sideways.

Crab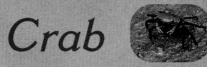

A quick sideways glance,
A brief soft-shoe over sand.
I scuttle away.

Caterpillar

How slow and hairy
Am I over the long grass.
Someday I will change.

A wormlike creature, the caterpillar is
really the second, or larval, stage of a
moth's or butterfly's life. A caterpillar's
body is made up of thirteen rings or
segments, not including its head. When
it moves, the caterpillar guides itself by
a pair of jointed feelers.

Butterfly

Can you paint a psalm?
Can you wallpaper a dream?
I can—with my wings.

butterfly

The butterfly, a daytime flier, is attracted to the bright flowers in a garden. It belongs to the Lepidoptera order, a name that comes from two Greek words—lepido, or scale, and pteron, or wing. The wings are covered with scales that are so tiny that they look like dust.

13

chipmunk

Chipmunk

I play peekaboo,
  Hide-and-seek, catch-as-catch-can.
  Heads up! Here I am.

*The chipmunk is a ground
dweller and lives in underground
tunnels, where it stores its food—
mostly nuts and seeds. It has
expandable cheek pouches for
carrying food back to its burrow.*

Grasshopper

I am UFO,
Making landfall on a stem.
What alien eyes.

grasshopper

A grasshopper is an herbivore, which means it eats only plants. It has five eyes and six legs. A grasshopper is able to leap twenty times the length of its own body.

Squirrel

You say, "What a tail!
What beady eyes! What quick steps!"
I say, "Nuts to you."

*The squirrel has a flexible body, well adapted for
its life in trees. Its bushy tail is used for balance;
the sharp, curved claws help grip tree trunks.*

Dragonfly

Sun through stained-glass wings
Throws shadows on a grass stem.
My flight is a hymn.

dragonfly

Tiny veins crisscross inside a dragonfly's wings, which make them sturdy. The dragonfly almost never walks. It uses its legs to rest on stems or catch its prey.

Spider

I spin out my life,
Strand after strand of pure silk.
Touch it if you dare.

*Spiders have eight legs. Although all spiders
have silk-producing glands near the back end
of their abdomens, not all spiders spin webs.*

Lizard

I am green as grass,
Green as moss, miracles, morn,
Green as a moment.

lizard

A lizard is a scaly-skinned
reptile. Cold-blooded, it must
bask in the sun to raise its body
temperature enough to keep active.

25

Hummingbird

Do hummingbirds dream
Of soaring on eagle wings?
Just for a moment.

The smallest bird in the world is in the hummingbird family. Hummingbirds live only in the Western Hemisphere. The hummingbird's name comes from the humming sound made by its wings. Some small hummingbirds can beat their wings as many as eighty times a second.

hummingbird

Turtle

Anywhere I go
I carry my home with me:
My standard shelter.

turtle

The turtle is a reptile easily recognized by its shell. The upper shell is called the carapace and covers the turtle's back. The bottom part, or plastron, protects the turtle's belly. Turtles have no teeth, but their beaks have sharp edges to cut food.

Tree Frog

I am a one-hop-
to-freedom kind of creature,
Once I can let go.

tree frog

Most tree frogs have suctionlike pads on their feet to help them climb. Like all frogs, the tree frog does not have a rib cage surrounding its internal organs. That is why, if you pick it up, a frog feels soft-bellied.

Baby

We walk hand in hand,
My fingers signaling *trust*,
Yours telling me *love*.

baby

*The hands belong to my daughter, Heidi, and her
first baby, Maddison Jane, now eight years old.*